REGINALD T. STELLE

52 powerful prosperity promises

REGINALD T. STEELE

52 powerful prosperity promises

HUNTER ENTERTAINMENT NETWORK

Colorado Springs, Colorado

52 Powerful Prosperity Promises
Copyright © 2017 by Reginald T. Steele
First Edition: January 2017

To order products, or for any other correspondence:

Hunter Entertainment Network
4164 Austin Bluffs Parkway, Suite 214
Colorado Springs, Colorado 80918
Tel. (253) 906-2160 – Fax: (719) 358-9051
E-mail: contact@hunter-entertainment.com
Or reach us on the internet: www.hunter-entertainment.com
"Offering God's Heart to a Dying World"

This book and all other Hunter Heart Publishing™, Hunter Heart Kids™ and Eagle's Wings Press™ products are available at Christian bookstores and distributors worldwide.

Chief Editor: Gord Dormer
Book cover design: Phil Coles Independent Design
Layout & logos: Exousia Marketing Group www.exousiamg.com

ISBN: 978-1-937741-31-0
Printed in the United States of America

TABLE OF CONTENTS

INTRODUCTION

Growing up in church, I would regularly hear this phrase from the preacher – "God wants you to have holy hands and empty pockets." Even as I child, I would question why a God that was described as loving and kind would want me to be without money? I would wonder to myself, if God created us, why would He not want us to have money to take care of His creation?

It wasn't until later in life, as I continued to grow in my relationship with the Lord, did I realize that the view of money had been twisted by the preacher who was delivering the message. Sometimes, we can accidently put limitations on God when it comes to our finances, because of our own personal experiences and stubborn mindsets.

Maybe that man of God found it too hard to believe that the Lord wanted financial abundance to come into his life, because he felt as though he did not deserve it. Maybe he had believed before, but felt let down because the overflow took too long to manifest. Maybe demographics and economics became more believable than the reality that God could supernaturally pull his congregation out of the grip of poverty. Whatever the reasoning was, I refused to give into the belief that holy living equated to needy living.

For too long, prosperity has been looked at negatively by the church. The favor of God (blessings and abundance) has been prepared for the people of God. The view of the God we serve must be shifted from a cheap, stingy, impoverished Master to a Father that wants to provide, faithfully fund, and distribute His massive wealth to His children.

Here is the truth: our God is not barren and He is not broke. He is full of riches and wealth. He has enough to go around for His church. He wants us to tap into His abundance by believing in His Word and applying His principles to our way of thinking. It is our covenantal right to receive His promise! I have a desire to encourage the Body of Christ to believe that God has promised us a life of prosperity, meaning that He desires we live to advance, to make progress, to succeed, and to be profitable. God desires that we, as Christians, have a successful journey through life.

In order for you to start this journey, let's look at the father of our faith, Abram (who later became Abraham). Knowing his history can help us understand our destiny.

Genesis 13:2: "Abram was very rich in livestock, in silver, and in gold."

The father of our faith is described as a very wealthy man. He was not just rich, he was very (extremely, exceeding, immensely, tremendously, and hugely) rich. As Christians, we not only inherit his faith, we inherit his wealth, as well. Why is wealth needed? I'm glad you asked! Abundant living is the fruit of being connected to a prosperous God. A wealthy life displays the wealth of God. All of your successes, accomplishments, increase, and advantages are to do one thing only, bring Him glory. Giving God glory means to boast and brag about what He has done for you!

The inheritance of Abraham does not stop in the Old Testament. It continues in the New Testament, as well. Because of Jesus Christ, the lines of division have been eradicated. Cultural and racial walls have been dissolved because of Jesus. We have the blessed ability to take part in His covenant.

Galatians 3:14: "... the blessing of Abraham might come upon the Gentiles in Christ Jesus that we might receive the promise of the spirit through faith."

The same blessing of an abundance of cattle, silver, and gold (an abundance of wealth and possessions) has been made available to us because of Christ. But the promise can only be received by faith. If you can have faith in God for salvation, healing, and restoration, you must also have faith in God for His divine prosperity for your life. If you believe that God does not want you to be sick in your body, you must have the same belief that God does not want you to always struggle in the finance department. If you find it difficult to believe for wealth and riches from God, it is okay to ask Him to help you with your unbelief. If you feel as though you do not deserve a blessed life from God, remember that the purpose of Jesus going to the Cross was not just to offer you salvation. He not only went to the Cross to redeem us from sin, but also from the curse of the law, which included poverty. (2 Corinthians 8:9). Jesus became poor for us, so that we could enjoy His prosperity.

Galatians 3:29: "And if you are Christ's, then you are Abraham's seed, and heirs according to the promise."

When you confess Jesus as your Lord and Savior, you are saying you belong to Him. That connection to Christ also includes a spiritual connection to Abraham. He was the original recipient of the promise of wealth and riches. We are the continuation of that promise. We are heirs; meaning, we are legally entitled to the legacy and property of another. God's promise to the father of our faith has been legally transferred to us by the blood of Jesus Christ. If you say you belong to Christ, you are saying prosperity, abundance, increase, overflow, wealth, and possessions belong to you!

As you read these 52 prosperity principles and promises, I pray you mix what you are reading with your faith. If you are struggling with seeing the blessings of God come into your life, I am believing that you will allow His Word to shift your perception of who God is and what He desires to do for you. If you are strong in your faith when it comes to His prosperity, I am hoping you will be encouraged to believe God for more. I want to see the people of God walk in the full manifestation of God's promise to us. Together, let's live a life of abundant living. Let's believe the promises and principles of prosperity!

52 POWERFUL PROSPERITY PROMISES

WEEK ONE

Psalm 118:25: "Save now, I pray O lord. O lord, I pray send now prosperity."

The psalmist was asking God to send prosperity now; meaning the present time or moment; very soon. God wants you to prosper in this day and time. The writer is putting a demand on His Word. He was asking for an immediate response from God. You can place a demand on God to immediately respond to your current situation.

WEEK TWO

Genesis 26:12-13: "Then Isaac, he sowed in the land and he reaped in the same year one-hundred fold. And the Lord blessed him. The man began to prosper. And he continued prospering until he became very prosperous."

It wasn't until Isaac sowed, or planted what he had in the ground, that God was able to multiply his seed. As modern day believers, we also have the responsibility to sow what we have into the Kingdom of God. Once you release your seed, God then has a responsibility to cause that seed to multiply and will continue multiplying based upon what you release.

WEEK THREE

Deuteronomy 8:18: "And you shall remember the Lord your God, for it is He who gives you power to get wealth, that He may establish His covenant which He swore to your fathers, as it is this day."

God has given you the strength, the means, the substance, the endurance, the capacity, and the ability to create wealth. It does not matter if you are a business owner or an employee. He has given you the ability to work, and to work well. God desires that we gain wealth for one purpose only, to establish His covenant promise of prosperity.

WEEK FOUR

Isaiah 1:19: "If you are willing and obedient, You shall eat the good of the land;"

When you are ready, eager, and prepared to live a continual life in His will, He will make sure that your needs and desires are met. He will adequately provide for you by choosing His will over yours.

When you make the decision to submit, or yield, to the ways of the Lord, He promises you will live a high-quality life full of satisfaction that can only come from Him.

WEEK FIVE

John 10:10b: "... I have come that they may have life, and that they may have it more abundantly."

Before Christ, life was empty, void, and always a struggle. With Christ, you finally feel alive. The purpose of Jesus coming to the earth was not just to save you. It was to allow you to live an abundant life. This means a life that is overflowing, full of surplus, over and above the average, more than enough, profuse, extraordinary, and a more-than-sufficient life! Thank the Lord for His ever-flowing supply He has given you with His salvation.

WEEK SIX

Psalm 115:13: "He will bless those who fear the Lord, Both small and great."

When you have a level of respect and reverence for God, it causes Him to bless (show special favor toward) you. Not only will He bless your life in a big way, but He will also take care of the small details of your life. It's not the amount or size of the blessing that matters. It's the fact that God promises to provide a well-rounded, balanced life full of blessings.

WEEK SEVEN

Ecclesiastes 10:19: "A feast is made for laughter, And wine makes merry; But money answers everything."

God has a developed an economic system of exchange of buying and selling that requires money to be used, in order for the exchange to take place. Because of this, it is true in every sense of Scripture. Money is necessary to thrive in this life. No matter what country you live in, a monetary system exists.

WEEK EIGHT

Ecclesiastes 7:12: "For wisdom is a defense as money is a defense, But the excellence of knowledge is that wisdom gives life to those who have it."

Money is not just used as a monetary gift of exchange, it is used to shield you and protect you from poverty. If you have money to buy a home, you will not be homeless. If you have money to buy food, you will not go hungry. As your economic status increases, so does your ability to live in better neighborhoods, attend better schools, and ultimately, improve your quality of life.

WEEK NINE

Philippians 4:19: "And my God shall supply all your need according to His riches in glory by Christ Jesus."

Without a doubt, God will meet your needs and make your wants available. He has a supply that will never run out. He is the God of more than enough. He provides us with the tangible and the intangible. Because the Lord owns everything, there is no lack in Him. His wealth is massive and He desires to supply it to you!

WEEK TEN

Psalm 35:27: "Let the Lord be magnified, Who has pleasure in the prosperity of His servant."

The Lord enjoys seeing His people prosper. That means He is satisfied, fulfilled, and happy to see you succeed in every area of your life. When you live a prosperous life, not only do you fill His heart with joy, but you magnify the Lord. Living in His prosperity makes God bigger to those who are observing your life.

WEEK ELEVEN

Psalm 34:10: "... But those who seek the Lord shall not lack any good thing."

Those who eagerly pursue the Lord live an abundant, prosperous life. When you make it your life's purpose to go after God, His Word, and His ways, you have no choice but to live a life where lack does not exist. He promises there is no shortage in Him. He will be the God of more than enough when you seek Him.

WEEK TWELVE

Psalm 23:1: "The Lord is my shepherd; I shall not want."

The Lord is also called the Shepherd; One who protects, covers, and guides His people. When you trust the Lord to oversee your life, He will lead you into a life where there is no famine. There is no desire- physical, emotional, or spiritual- that He will not provide for you when you follow Him. Allow God to show you the way. Trust that He will escort you into a life of prosperity.

WEEK THIRTEEN

Psalm 23:5: "... My cup runs over..."

God wants you to have a life of overflow; a life of surplus. When He gives you enough for yourself, the overflow should be for others. He has a way of blessing you with so much that you have no choice but to allow others to partake in the blessing. He wants your life to run over with spiritual and financial blessings- enough that you have to give it away.

WEEK FOURTEEN

Exodus 23:25: "So you serve the Lord your God and He will bless your bread and your water."

Serving the Lord opens the window of Heaven over your life. Because you are performing duties for Him, He will make sure that your physical needs are met. When you support the things of God, He will bless you with food and drink – the necessities of life. If you take care of the things of God, He will make sure you are taken care of.

WEEK FIFTEEN

Job 36:11: "If they obey and serve Him, they shall spend their days in prosperity and their years in pleasures."

Making the choice to obey and serve the Lord comes with wonderful conditions. God promises that you will have a life full of prosperity. You create a calendar filled with appointments of abundance. You will start and end your day with success. And those days turn into years that are gratifying and fulfilling all because you made a choice to obey and serve the Lord.

WEEK SIXTEEN

Proverbs 13:22: "A good man leaves an inheritance to his children's children. But the wealth of the sinner is stored up for the righteous…"

It is a blessing to leave behind a legacy of provision for your children and grandchildren. The prosperity of God will not only allow you to live a blessed life, but it will continue for generations. Wealth gained by those who choose not to serve the Lord usually ends in selfish gain and heartless plans. Because God is sovereign, He has a way to cause the sinner's wealth to be used for God's purposes anyway.

WEEK SEVENTEEN

Proverbs 28:20: "A faithful man will abound in blessings."

A faithful life equals a blessed life. Having stability in your life produces prosperity. Living a steadfast, stable life in Christ positions you to receive His best. Your faithfulness to Him will cause your life to thrive, flourish, and multiply in abundance. The Lord will allow you to advance in ways you would never imagine, simply because you are faithful to Him.

WEEK EIGHTEEN

2 Chronicles 20:20: "Believe in the Lord your God and you will be established. Believe in His prophets and you shall prosper."

Acknowledging God as your Lord means that He is the master, ruler, and ultimate head of your life. Coming to that conclusion allows for a settled life, because you are firmly rooted in Him. God has placed prophets (Pastors) in the earth to preach and teach the Word of God to strengthen your bond with Him, as the Lord of your life. This will ultimately cause you to prosper in your relationship with Him.

WEEK NINETEEN

Proverbs 3:9-10: "Honor the Lord with your possessions, And with the firstfruits of all your increase; So your barns will be filled with plenty, And your vats will overflow with new wine."

In order to continue to live a life of prosperity, you must give credit to the One who has blessed you. He is the One who has caused you to possess, acquire, and obtain His blessing. He is the One who causes it to continue to increase. When you praise the prosperity giver, He allows His abundance to continue in your life. Your home will be full and your supply will never run out.

WEEK TWENTY

3 John 1:2: "Beloved, I wish above all things that you may prosper and be in good health even as your soul prospers."

It is the desire of God that you be whole and complete in every area of your life. This means that you prosper in your finances, emotions, and your physical health. God knows that we need money to purchase the necessities of life like food, clothing, and shelter. He knows that our emotional well-being is important to maintain healthy, loving relationships with others. He also knows that our body needs to be in good, working order to fulfill His purpose. He strongly wants us to prosper, not when we get to Heaven, but while we are here on Earth.

WEEK TWENTY-ONE

Psalm 1:2-3: "But his delight is in the law of the Lord, And in His law he meditates day and night. He shall be like a tree planted by the rivers of water, That brings forth its fruit in its season, Whose leaf also shall not wither; And whatever he does shall prosper."

Finding enjoyment in the ways of God will cause you to study His Word more and more. When you develop the habit of reading the Bible, your life becomes stable and healthy. You will maintain an abundant life overflowing with good fruit; and the fruit will be enjoyed by those who see it and by those who taste it. There will be a freshness that will attract others to the God in you. So much that whatever you do; and wherever you go, you will have good success.

WEEK TWENTY-TWO

Psalm 37:25: "I have been young, and now am old; yet I have not seen the righteous forsaken nor His seed begging bread."

It doesn't matter what stage of life you are in, you will never see His children in a state of abandonment, only abundance. Because you belong to God, He cannot leave you or turn His back on you; not only spiritually, but financially. He will not allow you to come to a financial bottom where you have to beg from strangers. No matter what you are facing financially, trust the God of more than enough to provide for you. He does not just have to, He wants to.

WEEK TWENTY-THREE

Malachi 3:10: "Bring all the tithes into the storehouse, That there may be food in My house, And try Me now in this," Says the Lord of hosts, "If I will not open for you the windows of heaven and pour out for you such blessing that there will not be room enough to receive it."

God blesses you so you can bless His house (His church). Because our world is built on a monetary system, He has instructed His people to return a small portion (10%) of their abundance to the church. God challenges you to do so and then promises that He will rain down more prosperity over your life – so much that you will have to give it away! Allow the window to be opened over your life by blessing His house.

WEEK TWENTY-FOUR

Joshua 1:8: "This Book of the Law shall not depart from your mouth, but you shall meditate in it day and night, that you may observe to do according to all that is written in it. For then you will make your way prosperous, and then you will have good success."

When you refuse to withdraw from the Word of God, He promises two amazing things. Your life will not only be prosperous, it will be successful. You can be economically wealthy, but have damaged personal relationships with others. Or you can be swimming in bills and debt, but have a strong family unit of support. When you not only read the Word of God, but do the Word of God, He will allow you to have a financially abundant life and blessed personal life, as well. Your way of living will be blessed, as well as your life with others.

WEEK TWENTY-FIVE

Psalm 112:2-3: "His descendants will be mighty on earth; The generation of the upright will be blessed. Wealth and riches will be in his house, And his righteousness endures forever."

God wants His people to be strong physically and morally. Living an upright life consists of making good, God-like decisions that will ultimately produce blessings in your life. When you live a God-decision life, financial abundance will come to your house. He has a financial plan set up for those He calls His own. Making the decision to follow Him will bring wealth and riches to you and your loved ones.

WEEK TWENTY-SIX

Luke 6:38: "Give, and it will be given to you: good measure, pressed down, shaken together, and running over will be put into your bosom. For with the same measure that you use, it will be measured back to you."

Giving is the key to seeing continued prosperity in your life. It is the will of God that you release a portion of what you have earned back into the Kingdom. When you give, He makes sure you get a return that is much more than what you gave. God supernaturally multiplies what you give based upon how much you give to Him.

WEEK TWENTY-SEVEN

Psalm 84:11: "... No good thing will He withhold from those who walk uprightly..."

The prosperity of God is connected to your lifestyle. God has promised that when you choose to live an upright life- a life that is stable, steady, and connected to Him- He will allow good things to be released into your life. If you choose not to walk upright, it is possible that you make Him unable to release what is in His hand for you. Walking upright will release your prosperity. Live according to the Word of God, so His abundance will flow freely in your life.

WEEK TWENTY-EIGHT

Proverbs 10:22: "The blessing of the Lord makes one rich, And He adds no sorrow with it."

God blessing you means that He has released special favor upon you. Wealth, affluence, prosperity, and inexhaustible resources are attached to His favor. When the blessing comes from the Lord, it is a time to rejoice. It is not time to worry or fear that what He has given you will somehow diminish. He does not add depression, sadness, or worry to it. He wants you to enjoy living a *well to do* life.

WEEK TWENTY-NINE

Matthew 6:33: "But seek first the kingdom of God and His righteousness, and all these things shall be added to you."

What you have right now is not good enough with the Lord. He wants to add things to your life. Not just spiritual things, but tangible items that we need every day. A home to live in, a car to drive, and the list goes on and on. God does not mind if you have things, as long as things do not have you! When you seek His Kingdom (His rule and authority) and His righteousness (right way of living) first, He will begin to add things to you, because He knows you will always keep Him as your first priority.

WEEK THIRTY

Deuteronomy 28:2: "And all these blessings shall come upon you and overtake you, because you obey the voice of the Lord your God."

Prosperity is linked to your obedience to God. There is a blessing that comes with obeying His voice (the Word of God). He promises when you execute His will, He will allow blessings to not only catch up with you, but run you over!

WEEK THIRTY-ONE

Deuteronomy 1:11: "May the Lord God of your fathers make you a thousand times more numerous than you are, and bless you as He has promised you."

God is a generational God. He made a promise to our father in the faith, Abraham, a long time ago. A promise of success and abundant living. Today, we are still able to receive the promise that has been multiplied! God desires that you have an even greater quantity than what was promised to our forefathers. He wants His blessings to snowball, becoming more numerous than ever before!

WEEK THIRTY-TWO

Deuteronomy 28:8: "The Lord will command the blessing on you in your storehouses and in all to which you set your hand, and He will bless you in the land which the Lord your God is giving you."

When abundant blessings visit you, it is because of the Lord's command. The Lord will instruct prosperity to visit the building where your goods are stored. A modern day storehouse could be your home, a storage unit where you have placed your abundance, or your bank account. To make it better, He will command His blessing on whatever you decide, or purpose, in your mind to do. He will bless your endeavors and keep you in the land He has given you for His glory.

WEEK THIRTY-THREE

Matthew 6:10: "Your kingdom come. Your will be done on earth as it is in heaven."

The Lord has made His heavenly prosperity available to His people here on Earth. There is no lack or want in Heaven. There are mansions and streets paved with gold in our future home. Jesus is our King. A king protects and provides for those in His Kingdom. You have the ability to pray to Him and ask for a king's life right now!

WEEK THIRTY-FOUR

Matthew 5:5: "Blessed are the meek, For they shall inherit the earth."

Being meek means to be submissive, humble, and yielding. In the things of God, meekness is not a weakness. It is a great strength. Jesus says that those who have this character trait shall (without doubt) receive the Earth. Everything comes from the Earth. For example, a seed is planted in the Earth. The tree grows and is cut down to be a house. Another example: metal is an element found in the Earth. The metal is melted and molded into a car. The Word of God says we were created from dust. Dust comes from the Earth. Living a meek life means that everything you see is yours!

WEEK THIRTY-FIVE

Proverbs 20:7: "The righteous man walks in his integrity; His children are blessed after him."

God's prosperity is not just for you; it is for your children. His blessings will affect the generation after you when you not only talk the talk, but walk the walk. Walking in integrity means to pursue a course of action or way of life that is honest, upright, sincere, and truthful. Your children are blessed, not just because of God's blessings, but because they are watching your life. Children mimic what they see. Watching you live an integral life will cause them to do the same.

WEEK THIRTY-SIX

Ecclesiastes 7:14: "In the day of prosperity be joyful, But in the day of adversity consider: Surely God has appointed the one as well as the other, So that man can find out nothing that will come after him."

God has designed days of success and abundance for you. And He reminds you to enjoy those days. Rejoice, celebrate, and give Him praise for them. But He also appoints challenging days, as well. You do not have to let those days belittle the great things He has done for you. No matter what you face, refuse to allow the appointed days of difficulty affect the assigned days of prosperity that are soon to come.

WEEK THIRTY-SEVEN

Matthew 7:11: "If you then, being evil, know how to give good gifts to your children, how much more will your Father who is in heaven give good things to those who ask Him."

Saying you are a child of God means that you acknowledge Him as your Father. As His child, you are expected to ask Him for whatever you need. Just as you would reward your child, He wants to do the same. And because He is the perfect parent, He will give you more than you could ever hope for.

WEEK THIRTY-EIGHT

Ephesians 3:20: "Now to Him who is able to do exceedingly abundantly above all that we ask or think..."

Prosperity comes from the power of God. He is always looking for an opportunity to bless you with more than what your limited mind can dream. Because of His blessed abundance, He will always outmatch what you ask for. He will eclipse your thoughts of success with His idea of opulence. He will exceed your imagination and give you more than enough.

WEEK THIRTY-NINE

Psalm 115:14: "May the Lord give you increase more and more, You and your children."

God is a God of increase, growth, and enlargement. He wants you to gain, not lose. He wants you to progress, not regress. He wants you to advance in every way. Because you belong to Him, He desires that you have a flourishing livelihood. Allow Him the opportunity to fulfill His ambition. Grant the Lord permission not only to prosper your life, but the life of your children, as well.

WEEK FORTY

Romans 13:8: "Owe no one anything except to love one another..."

The prosperity of God will get you out of debt. His overflow will cover the outstanding balance you once owed. Your financial obligation will be paid by the constant flow of increase He releases into your life. His abundance will get you out of the hole. Your love for others will be the only thing you are required to pay back.

WEEK FORTY-ONE

Proverbs 10:4: "He who has a slack hand becomes poor, But the hand of the diligent makes rich."

The Lord wants all of His children to prosper. But His prosperity can be hindered if you choose to be inactive. Your passive approach to work can slow down His ability to manifest. Decide to be hardworking and eager at your place of employment. When you are persistently pursuing a prosperous life, wealth will come your way.

WEEK FORTY-TWO

2 Corinthians 9:7-8: "So let each one give as he purposes in his heart, not grudgingly or of necessity; for God loves a cheerful giver. And God is able to make all grace abound toward you, that you, always having all sufficiency in all things, may have an abundance for every good work."

When you happily release finances into the Kingdom of God, the Lord delights in it. Simply giving back a small portion of what you have earned gets His attention and causes Him to release His unmerited favor directed toward you. He will give you more to work with, because you have refused to hold back. Because your heart has His purpose in mind, He will cause success to head your way!

WEEK FORTY-THREE

Ecclesiastes 11:1: "Cast your bread upon the waters, For you will find it after many days."

It takes faith to give your substance away. It can be a challenging thing to send off your provision not knowing where it could end up. But God is the Lord of everything; He controls the ebb and flow of life. He will make sure that what you give to Him will return. Maybe not immediately, but exactly when you need it. His prosperity will cause your sustenance to return after a while.

WEEK FORTY-FOUR

Genesis 8:22: "While the earth remains, seedtime and harvest, cold and heat, winter and summer, And day and night shall not cease."

God has created a successful system that sustains us here on Earth. This system is called seasons. The times of the year have been governed by God and cannot take place without each other. There is also a season when you give. Sowing financially into the Kingdom of God is your seedtime. God will multiply your monetary seed and produce an abundant harvest based upon what you put into His fertile ground. And the process will not come to an end as long as the Earth remains.

WEEK FORTY-FIVE

Deuteronomy 28:12: "The Lord will open to you His good treasure, the heavens, to give the rain to your land in its season, and to bless all the work of your hand. You shall lend to many nations, but you shall not borrow."

God will open His heavenly abundance over your life. He will drench your region by showering down His blessings in the right place; at the right time. Your labor will not be in vain, because He will anoint your efforts. His abundance causes you to be like a bank, always granting loans for others and living on the interest of His divine supply.

WEEK FORTY-SIX

Jeremiah 29:11: "For I know the thoughts that I think toward you, says the Lord, thoughts of peace and not of evil, to give you a future and a hope."

When the Lord thinks about you, His thoughts are not unpleasant. His thoughts are not destructive, disastrous, or depraved. His attention is placed on ways He can bless your life in every way. He wants a life for you where nothing is missing; nothing broken. He wants your life to be whole and complete in Him for today and for your days to come.

WEEK FORTY-SEVEN

Psalm 128:2: "When you eat the labor of your hands, You shall be happy, and it shall be well with you."

When God has opened up an opportunity for you to work, He has unlocked a way to bless you through employment. Earning a paycheck allows you to purchase what you need to live. When He has allowed your skill, ability, or talent to be compensated with money, you should find pleasure and contentment in the gratifying grace of God.

WEEK FORTY-EIGHT

Genesis 39:2-3: "The Lord was with Joseph, and he was a successful man; and he was in the house of his master the Egyptian. And his master saw that the Lord was with him and that the Lord made all he did to prosper in his hand."

When the Lord is amidst you, other people can see it. When God has surrounded your life, how can you have anything less than success? God has a way of touching your life with so much good fortune that those who may not know of Him will eventually want to. Remember, when the Lord pushes His benefits toward you, it could be for those around you.

WEEK FORTY-NINE

Matthew 6:3-4: "But when you do a charitable deed, do not let your left hand know what your right hand is doing, that your charitable deed may be in secret; and your Father who sees in secret will Himself reward you openly."

Because God has blessed your life with so much, you don't have to go around bragging to others about what you have obtained or accomplished. The Lord wants you to give Spirit-led assistance and to contribute to others who may be in need. Shouting out your charitable deeds to others will only give you a temporary and self-seeking type of payment. When you keep your good deeds *hush-hush*, God will bless you with a bonus so big everyone cannot help but see it.

WEEK FIFTY

Luke 18:29-30: "So He said to them, "Assuredly, I say to you, there is no one who has left house or parents or brothers or wife or children, for the sake of the kingdom of God, who shall not receive many times more in this present time, and in the age to come eternal life."

Prosperity can be a hard concept to grasp, especially by others who have raised you or who have known you for a long time. Leaving a certain mindset or culture can seem difficult, because successful living can seem like an unachievable goal based upon your family history. When you journey into the Kingdom of God, you will have the same desire as Him- to live an abundant life. Making the decision to shift to His prosperity will allow you to acquire His wealth, not when you get to Heaven, but right now, while you live on Earth.

WEEK FIFTY-ONE

Matthew 25:23: "... 'Well done, good and faithful servant; you have been faithful over a few things, I will make you ruler over many things...'"

The Lord expects you to be loyal to His blessing, small or great. He is watching how you take care of what He has given you. He is checking on you to see if you are reliable, dependable, and devoted to what He has provided. When you are constant in tending to His contributions to your life, He will cause you to reign over more than you had before.

WEEK FIFTY-TWO

Ecclesiastes 5:19: "As for every man to whom God has given riches and wealth, and given him power to eat of it, to receive his heritage and rejoice in his labor—this is the gift of God."

When God has given you the strength to work and earn money and possessions, you have entered into the ancestry of our Father. He has endowed you with the ability to create abundance. His affluence is purposed to add great joy to your life. He is waiting to give away His abundant commodities and add them to your diligent endeavors. What an amazing allowance that the God of more than enough has released to you!

About the Author

Pastor Reginald Steele is the Founder and Senior Pastor of *Kingdom in the Valley Christian Church*, a twelve-year-old ministry dedicated to building God's Kingdom one family at a time. His teaching and preaching is both practical and powerful, encouraging men and women of God to live up to their full potential in Christ. Under his leadership, Kingdom is considered one of the fastest growing churches in Phoenix, Arizona. Over 12,000 people of all races, ages, and backgrounds call *Kingdom* their church home.

Pastor Reginald has been married to his high school sweetheart, Kelley Steele, for over twenty years and is a dedicated father to their five young adult children.

BOOKS BY
REGINALD T. STEELE

Available online at www.hunter-entertainment.com
and Amazon.com.

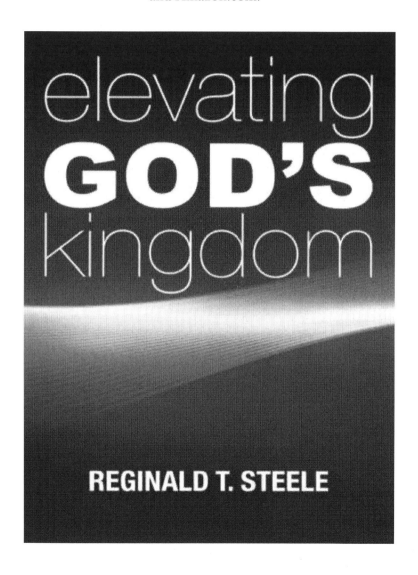

BOOKS BY
REGINALD T. STEELE

Available online at www.hunter-entertainment.com
and Amazon.com.

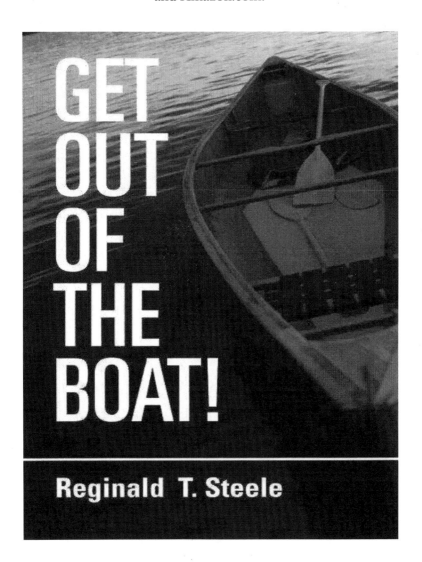

KINGDOM

KVCC ADMINISTRATIVE OFFICE

Kingdom is a non-denominational, multi-cultural church.

11640 N. 19th Ave
Phoenix AZ 85029

Business Phone: (602) 441-0540

Business Fax: (602) 795-8011

Email us at Info@kivcc.org

Service Times
Sunday:
8:00 a.m. (Family Service - no childcare or youth ministry)
9:30 a.m.
11:30 a.m.
Wednesday:
7:00 p.m.